Clothes Around the World

Sportswear

Jane Bingham

WAYLAND

First published in 2008 by Wayland

Copyright © Wayland 2008

Wayland
Hachette Children's Books
338 Euston Road
London NW1 3BH

Wayland Australia
Level 17/207 Kent Street
Sydney NSW 2000

Series editor: Joyce Bentley
Designer: Holly Fullbrook
Picture researcher: Kathy Lockley

British Library Cataloguing in Publication Data
Bingham, Jane
    Sportswear. - (Clothes around the world)
    1. Sports clothes - Juvenile literature
    I. Title
    391

ISBN 978 0 7502 5311 6

Printed in China

Wayland is a division of Hachette Children's Books,
an Hachette Livre UK company.

Contents

Why do people wear sportswear?

When people decide to play a sport, they usually change into different clothes. Sometimes they just put on special shoes, but often they dress up in a complete sports outfit. So why do people wear special clothes for sports?

Ice hockey players need lots of protection and goalkeepers need the most protection of all.

The most important reason for wearing sports clothes is safety. Proper sports equipment gives your body extra support. Sportswear can prevent you from injuring yourself. It can also protect you if you have an accident.

Wearing good sportswear makes you feel comfortable. It also helps you play your sport really well.

It Works!

Soccer strips

Soccer strips are the shirts and shorts worn by all the players in a team. Modern strips are lightweight and comfortable to wear. The bold strip colours make players easy to spot, so playing as a team becomes much easier. Wearing their strip makes the players feel proud of their team – and their supporters like wearing it too!

Sportswear around the world

Today, most sports are **international**, but there are still a few **national** sports. These sports have their own special clothes.

In Japan, sumo wrestlers wear brightly coloured padded belts. Sumo belts are made from around nine metres (30 feet) of silk. The silk is wrapped several times around the wrestler's body and fastened at the back in a large knot.

Before a wrestling match begins, sumo wrestlers parade around the ring in a special apron.

American rodeo riders dress like cowboys and cowgirls from the **Wild West**.

In Mexico, rodeo riding is very popular. Male rodeo riders wear a short jacket and tight trousers. They also have a wide-brimmed hat, called a sombrero. Women riders usually wear a **traditional** riding dress, with a very wide skirt and puffed sleeves.

The history of sportswear

By the time of the ancient Egyptians, people were playing a range of sports. Egyptian sports included boxing, running and gymnastics. The Egyptians did not have special sportswear. They wore cotton tunics and went barefoot.

In Roman times, **gladiators** fought each other as a kind of sport. Gladiators wore metal helmets, leg guards and arm guards. The rest of their body was left bare.

In **medieval times,** knights on horseback fought pretend battles known as jousts. They were protected by metal suits of armour.

Jousting knights hit each other with poles. But they were usually unhurt.

The ancient Maya people of Mexico played a violent game with a very hard ball. They wore a padded leather belt and helmet, with leather guards on their elbows and legs.

It Doesn't Work!

Sitting sideways
Until the 1920s, most women wore dresses to go horse riding. They rode side-saddle with both their legs on one side of the horse. This was very dangerous and they often fell off.

In **Tudor times**, men played a kind of tennis. But they didn't change into special clothes. They wore shoes with heels and they didn't even take off their hats.

By the 1880s, people were enjoying the new sport of cycling. Men cyclists wore knickerbockers – trousers that reached to just below the knee. Women often put on bloomers to go cycling. Bloomers were long, baggy trousers that were worn underneath a skirt.

In the early days of cycling, people dressed in special clothes for the sport.

Women played tennis in long skirts and hats until the 1920s. Then a few brave women took off their hats and started to wear shorter skirts. It took another ten years before a woman dared to wear tennis shorts.

Weird and Wonderful

Swimming dresses

In the 1700s, women went swimming in long dresses. Some of these dresses had heavy weights sewn into their hems. The weights made swimming very difficult, but they stopped the dress from floating up to show the swimmer's legs!

Women wore bathing dresses until the 1920s. The women in this picture are even wearing stockings.

What are sports clothes made from?

Sportswear can be made from a wide range of materials, but one of the most useful fabrics is cotton. Many people choose cotton sports clothes because they are lightweight and feel cool to wear.

Modern sailing suits are warm and waterproof, but they are also easy to move in.

Sometimes people need special sports clothes to keep out rain and water. Climbers and sailors wear lightweight, waterproof jackets, made from man-made fabrics, such as **gore-tex.** These special fabrics allow some air to pass in and out, so the wearer doesn't get too hot.

Sports boots and gloves are often made from leather because it is tough but **flexible**. But nowadays plastic is sometimes used instead. Plastic is especially useful for making safety helmets that are light but strong.

Surfers and windsurfers spend a lot of time in cold water, so they need to keep warm. They wear wetsuits made from a special material called neophrene.

Neophrene is a mixture of nylon and rubber. It clings very tightly to the wearer's body. Wetsuits work by trapping a warm layer of water next to the skin, and keeping all the cold water out.

When surfers wear a wetsuit, they can stay in the sea for hours without getting cold.

Underwater divers wear very thick wetsuits. They also have rubber flippers and masks. Rubber is a very useful material because it can be moulded into any shape.

What Would You Wear?

If you were going hiking on a wet and windy day, would you wear a jacket made from:
A. Cotton
B. Gore-tex
C. Wool
D. Rubber

(Answer on page 31)

The swimmer is wearing a lycra swimsuit and a thin rubber swimming cap.

Lycra is often used for sportswear. It is light and stretchy and it dries very fast. Swimsuits, running shorts and exercise wear can all be made from lycra.

Winter sports

People who take part in winter sports need to stay warm and dry. **Skiers** and snowboarders wear waterproof jackets that are lined with special **insulation material**. The insulation allows the wearer to stay warm without getting hot and sticky.

Ski-racers wear tight-fitting suits made from lycra, with extra padding on the elbows and knees. These skin-tight suits have a smooth, **streamlined** shape, which means that the racers can move very fast through the air.

Luge racers need to be as streamlined as possible. They wear skin-tight lycra suits.

Ice-skaters need very strong boots to give their feet and ankles lots of support. Modern skating boots are made from tough plastic that holds the foot very firmly.

It Works!

Ski-jump suits

Ski-jumpers aim to stay in the air for as long as possible. To help them do this, they wear a loose-fitting suit made from a soft, spongy material. Once a ski-jumper has taken off, the suit fills with air. This allows the jumper to hang in the air for a little longer.

Ball sports

When you play ball games, you need strong footwear and loose-fitting clothes. You also need to wear protective clothing. Wearing the right clothing helps to keep you safe from injuries, either from the ball or from other players.

American football is an exciting game but it can be very rough. Underneath their shirts, footballers wear large shoulder pads. They also have lots of padding round their waist and legs.

American footballers wear a hard plastic helmet with metal bars covering the face.

Hockey players need to protect their legs from the other players' hockey sticks. So they wear thick pads underneath their socks.

Hockey goalkeepers wear padded leg guards and a helmet. They have boots with metal toes, so they can kick the ball away from the goal.

What Would You Wear?

You're playing a game of throw and catch with a small hard ball. Would you wear:
A. Football strip and boots
B. Elbow pads
C. Leather jacket and boots
D. Lightweight helmet and padded gloves

(Answer on page 31)

Hockey players need to protect their shins from injury.

For some ball games, players wear a hat. The hat shades their eyes and helps them to see the ball more easily. Baseball players wear a cotton cap with a large peak. Nowadays, baseball caps are popular all over the world.

Baseball players also use a wide leather glove to help them catch the ball. As well as making catching easier, the glove protects the catcher's hand from injury.

It Works!

Spiky shoes

Golfers need to grip the ground very firmly when they are hitting the ball. So golfing shoes have plastic spikes on the soles. The shoes can be fitted with spikes of different sizes, depending on the softness of the ground. This means that golfers can always get a good grip.

Baseball catchers wear gloves made from tough leather to protect their hands.

Until very recently, players of cricket and tennis always wore white. But now things are changing. Today, cricketers often wear brightly coloured outfits for one-day international matches.

Cricketers strap pads onto their legs and they wear a helmet to protect their face.

Judo and other martial arts

Sports that involve some kind of fighting are known as martial arts. Judo, karate and fencing are all examples of martial arts. They each have their own special outfit.

For judo and karate, contestants wear a cotton suit. The suit has drawstring trousers and a short jacket fastened by a belt. The colour of the belt shows the level of the wearer's skill.

Judo jackets need to be strong, because contestants often grab hold of them.

Fencers fight with very thin swords. Even though their swords are blunt, fencers still wear a protective suit. The suit is made from a strong material that cannot be pierced. The fencer's face is covered by a mask of fine wire **mesh**.

Kendo is an ancient form of fencing that is popular in Japan. Today's contestants still wear traditional costumes.

Flashback

Kendo knights
Kendo contestants wear long black costumes based on the armour of the Japanese samurai. The samurai were knights who fought fierce duels with each other. Now, they are remembered in the ancient sport of kendo.

Cycling and motor sports

People who take part in cycling and motor sports run the risk of having a serious accident. The most important part of their equipment is their helmet.

If a car crashes at high speed, it can easily burst into flames. So racing drivers dress in fire-resistant suits. They wear a helmet with a wide plastic **visor** to give them an all-round view of the road.

Racing drivers wear fireproof clothing that protects them from head to toe.

Weird and Wonderful

Airbag jacket
Recently, some motorbike jackets have been fitted with built-in airbags. The bags are designed to **inflate** in a crash, and protect the rider's body. This new invention seems amazing now, but it may save many lives.

Motorbike racers wear leather suits, gloves and boots. The thick, tough leather of their suit keeps the wind out. It also helps to protect riders who fall off their bikes.

Racing cyclists wear a tight-fitting lycra suit and a very lightweight helmet. Their helmets are specially designed to be as streamlined as possible.

Sports on horseback

When people go horse riding they need a strong pair of boots and a hard hat to protect their head. Often they wear special trousers to give them extra grip.

American rodeo riders wear cowboy hats and boots. Usually, they wear **chaps** over their jeans. Chaps are over-trousers made from soft, rough leather. They help the rider to grip the horse's sides.

It Doesn't Work!

Unhelpful hats

Cowboy hats can have two hard peaks at the top. The peaks are meant to protect the rider's head in case of falls. In fact, cowboy hats do not give much protection. It is much safer to wear a hard hat.

For show jumping events, riders wear high boots, and special trousers, called jodhpurs. Riders also wear a hard hat with a tough outer shell. Inside, the hat is lined with a soft, **shock-absorbent** fabric.

Most jodhpurs have rough leather patches inside the knees, next to the horse. The patches help the rider to grip tightly.

Design your own strip

Why not create a simple strip for you and your friends? It doesn't matter what sport you play – you can still look great in your very own strip.

You will need
* A T-shirt
* T-shirt paints
* Paper, crayons and pens to work out your ideas

Figure 1

1. First think up a **logo** for your strip. This could be a lacrosse stick, some swimming goggles, or even a ping-pong bat! The most important thing is to keep it simple.

Figure 2

2. Now decide what colours you want to use. It's best to stick to just two or three colours.

3. Practice your logo until you can draw it easily. Then use T-shirt paints to draw it onto the front of your shirt.

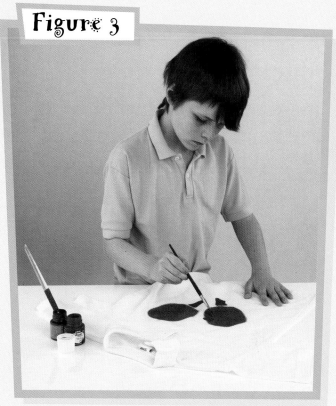

Figure 3

Figure 4

4. Now draw a big number on the back of your shirt. If you are making strips for lots of friends, you can all have different numbers on the back.

You can design a strip for almost any sport. What is your favourite sport?

Dress-up box

5-minute rodeo rider

American rodeo riders dress like cowboys. They wear leather chaps to protect their legs and use a rope lasso to catch cows.

To create your costume, you will need a pair of jeans and a shirt, a cowboy hat, a belt and a scarf. You will also need a large sheet of strong brown paper, scissors and tape.

1. Ask an adult to help cut a pair of chaps from brown paper.

2. Cut two paper fringes and tape along the outer edges of your chaps.

3. Tape your chaps to the top and sides of your jeans.

4. Now add a cowboy hat, scarf and belt.

Glossary

chaps – leather over-trousers worn by rodeo riders

flexible – able to bend easily

gladiators – Roman warriors who fought each other to entertain the public

gore-tex – a waterproof material with lots of tiny holes to let air in and out

inflate – fill with air

insulation material – material that traps warm air around the body

international –belonging to many countries

logo – a symbol that represents a team or a company

luge – a racing toboggan

lycra – a lightweight stretchy material that clings to the body

medieval times – a period of history between the years 1000 and 1450

mesh – a network of fine wires

national – belonging to one country

shock-absorbent – stopping any knocks or bumps from damaging the body

skiers – people who go skiing

streamlined –designed to move through air or water easily

traditional –used for hundreds of years

Tudor times – a period of English history between the years 1485 and 1603

visor – a see-through plastic covering for your eyes or face

Wild West – a period in the 1800s, when there were many cowboys herding cattle in west of the USA

What would you wear?

Answers to questions on pages 5 and 19.

Page 15
The best choice of material for your hiking jacket is B. Gore-tex is lightweight and waterproof and it keeps the wind out. Cotton would get soaked by the rain. Wool would protect you from the wind but it would soon become soggy and heavy. A rubber jacket would keep you dry and warm, but it would be heavy and hard to walk in.

Page 19
If you want to stay safe during your game of throw and catch you should wear D – a lightweight helmet and padded gloves. When a small, hard ball is flying around the most important part of your body to protect is your head. Padded gloves will stop you hurting your hands when you catch a hard ball.

Index

Photos or pictures are shown below in bold, **like this**.